HOW TO IMPROVE AT
FISHING

All the information you need to know to get on top of your game!

More than just instructional guides, the **HOW TO IMPROVE AT...** series gives you everything you need to achieve your goals — tips on technique, step-by-step demonstrations, nutritional advice, and the secrets of successful pro athletes. Excellent visual instructions and expert advice combine to act as your own personal trainer. These books aim to give you the know-how and confidence to improve your performance.

Studies have shown that an active approach to life makes you feel happier and less stressed. The easiest way to start is by taking up a new sport or improving your skills in an existing one. You simply have to choose an activity that enthuses you.

HOW TO IMPROVE AT FISHING does not promise instant success. It simply gives you the tools to become the best at whatever you choose to do.

Every care has been taken to ensure that these instructions are safe to follow, but in the event of injury Crabtree Publishing shall not be liable for any injuries or damages.

Andrew Walker was born and grew up in Norfolk, and was first taken fishing by his father at the age of four. He has been a passionate all-round angler ever since, enjoying the freedom of being close to nature and the relaxation and excitement that only fishing can bring. He now lives in Oxfordshire.

ticktock Media Ltd would like to thank the following for their help:

Katie

Matthew

Ievan

Josh

Ludlow Tackle, Ludlow, Shropshire
www.ludlowtackle.co.uk
Newlands Angling Club
www.newland-ac.org.uk
RS Baits, Eynsham, Oxfordshire
www.rsbaits.com
State Tackle, Witney, Oxfordshire
www.statetackle.co.uk

Crabtree Publishing Company
www.crabtreebooks.com

Author: Andrew Walker
Editors: John Crossingham, Annabel Savery
Proofreader: Adrianna Morganelli
Project coordinator: Robert Walker
Prepress technician: Margaret Amy Salter
Production coordinator: Margaret Amy Salter
Designer: Graham Rich
Managing Editor: Rachel Tisdale
Photographers: Chris Fairclough and Bobby Humphrey

Planning and production by Discovery Books Ltd.

Photo credits:

Matt Hayes: p. 47 (bottom)

Steve Partner: p. 47 (top)

Perth Museum and Art Gallery: p. 46 (right)

Walt Reynolds/www.fishingwithrolandmartin.com: p. 46 (left)

Andrew Walker: p. 4 (middle), 8 (top & middle), 9 (top), 45 (middle)

Library and Archives Canada Cataloguing in Publication

Walker, Andrew D., 1976-
    How to improve at fishing / Andrew D. Walker.

(How to improve at--)
Includes index.
ISBN 978-0-7787-3572-4 (bound).--ISBN 978-0-7787-3594-6 (pbk.)

    1. Fishing--Juvenile literature.
I. Title. II. Series: How to improve at--

SH445.W37 2009   j799.1   C2008-907841-1

Library of Congress Cataloging-in-Publication Data

Walker, Andrew D., 1976-
  How to improve at fishing / Andrew D. Walker.
      p. cm. -- (How to improve at--)
  Includes index.
   ISBN 978-0-7787-3594-6 (pbk. : alk. paper) -- ISBN 978-0-7787-3572-4
(reinforced library binding : alk. paper)
   1. Fishing--Juvenile literature. I. Title. II. Series.

SH445.W17 2009
799.1--dc22
                                2008052117

Crabtree Publishing Company
www.crabtreebooks.com   1-800-387-7650

Published in Canada
Crabtree Publishing
616 Welland Ave.
St. Catharines, Ontario
L2M 5V6

Published in the United States
Crabtree Publishing
PMB16A
350 Fifth Ave., Suite 3308
New York, NY 10118

CONTENTS

INTRODUCTION

Fishing, or angling, is one of the world's most popular participation sports. It is one of the only sports that's equally exciting and relaxing. Anyone, young or old, male or female, can fish, and anyone, no matter how inexperienced, can break a record.

Originally, people caught fish for food. These days we take great care to treat fish with respect and return them to the water completely unharmed. Catching fish is about learning the skills to outwit nature.

In this book are lots of hints and tips to help improve your angling skills. Remember, you don't need to catch lots of fish every time to enjoy fishing—you just need to respect nature and have a good time.

LOCATIONS & WHAT TO WEAR

*W*here you go fishing depends on the kind of waters found around where you live. If you're lucky you will have a choice of rivers, still waters (lakes and ponds), and maybe even the sea, too.

STILL WATERS

Still waters are enclosed bodies of water, such as lakes and ponds. They can be anything from a tiny farm pond or commercial fishery, to a huge glacial lake or water-filled gravel pit. There are many different species of fish and fishing tactics in still waters. It is usually more difficult to fish in larger still water lakes.

RIVERS

There are so many types of rivers to fish. Tiny little brooks may be home to just a few little trout and minnows. Big, powerful tidal rivers contain many more species. Still, you don't have to find the biggest rivers to find good angling. Even small streams are home to a lot of great fish.

THE SEA

The sea is a fantastic place to fish. You can lower a bait from a pier, cast a heavy weight hundreds of feet into turbulent water, or fish with a float off a rocky outcrop. If you happen to live near the sea, you are very lucky!

WHAT TO WEAR

When you go fishing you need to wear some sensible clothes. If it's cold, be sure to wear lots of layers.

WATERPROOF

Always carry waterproof clothing with you. You never know when it might rain!

DARK CLOTHES

Try and wear dark colored clothing. Bright colors can frighten the fish.

FOOTWEAR

Wear footwear with good grip. It can get muddy and slippery by the water's edge. *You could wear any sneakers or rainboots that have rubber soles.*

EQUIPMENT

Y*ou will probably start your fishing hobby with coarse fishing. Coarse fishing is fishing for freshwater fish which are not "game fish," such as trout or salmon. This style of angling uses a wide variety of skills and equipment depending on your location, the weather conditions and the time of year.*

EQUIPMENT

There are all sorts of fishing equipment (known as "tackle") available, including rods, reels, and lines. Many other bits and pieces are used for different species and situations.
The type of tackle used for a day's coarse fishing depends on where you are fishing and what you are hoping to catch. Here is a typical setup.

Umbrella
Chair
Tackle box
Bag
Weigh sling
Scales
Unhooking mat
Rod hold-all
Head torch

Landing net
Carp rod
Barbel rod with quiver-tip
Float rod
Rod rests
Rod bag

Reels

Catapult
Floats
Hooklength line

Fixed spool reels
Centerpin reel

TACKLE BOX

Much of the smaller equipment for coarse fishing is kept in a tackle box.

Hooks

Float rubbers
Used to attach river floats to the line.

Scales
For weighing fish.

Split-shot
Attached to the line when float fishing to weigh down the line. It makes the float sit upright in the water.

Hooklength material
For connecting your hook to your main line.

Scissors
For cutting line.

Lines
These can be monofilament or **braid**.

Disgorgers
Used for unhooking fish.

Floats
Floats come in different shapes and sizes.

Lures
Lures look like small fish that other fish want to eat.

Bait
Used to attract the fish.

Weights
Used in leger fishing to keep the hook near the bottom of the lake or river.

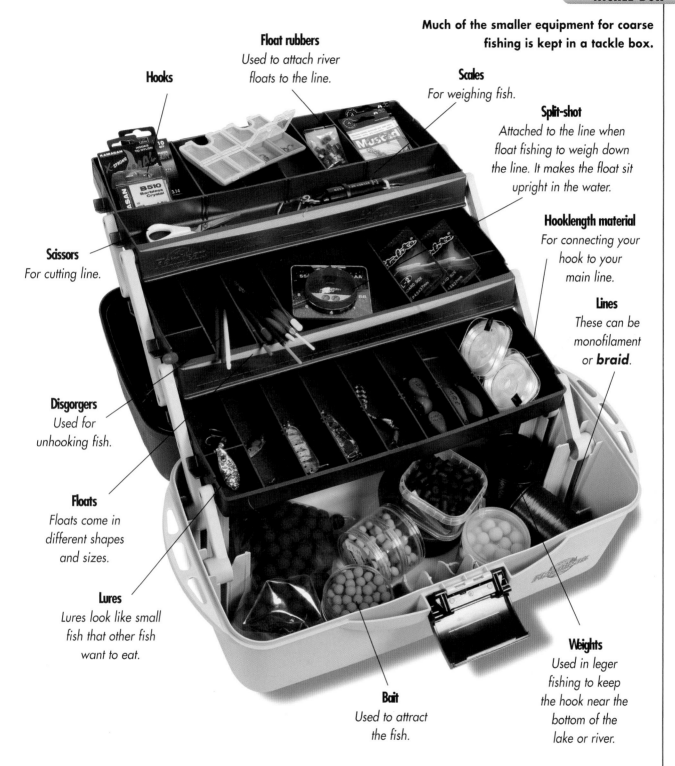

 TOP TIP
It's tempting to take as much tackle as possible for a day's fishing, but try to take as little as you can. That way, it's easier to move around as you follow the fish.

WATERCRAFT

Watercraft is your ability to "read the water," or figure out where the fish are and how to catch them.

FIND YOUR FISH

Take your time to observe the water before settling into a swim—this is the place where you fish. If the fish aren't there, you can't catch them!

What to look for

Some fish, like carp, chub and rudd, enjoy basking in the sun. On a warm day you can often see them very clearly. Tench, carp, bream, roach and crucians often roll or jump at the surface at dawn or dusk. Tench and carp also root about on the bottom when they're feeding—this sends clouds of mud and bubbles to the surface.

Look for trembling reeds or lilies, colored water (stirred up by fish on the bottom) and diving birds like grebes (below). These all indicate that fish are in the area.

Bubbles on the surface from feeding fish.

A chub basking in the sun.

A diving grebe.

Fish like cover from overhanging trees, reeds or weedbeds.

PREDATORS

You can see swirling of the water's surface when predatory fish like perch and pike are feeding on other fish. Remember that predators will be wherever prey fish are. Try to find schools of small fish by looking for diving birds and little fish near the surface.

WEATHER CONDITIONS

Watch the weather conditions where you're fishing. On a still water, a strong, warm wind blows insect life and other fish food goodies toward the bank and warms the water. It's often good to fish into a wind like this. If the wind is cold, however, it can chill the water. In this weather, it's usually best to fish in sheltered, deeper areas.

SNAGS

Snags like submerged trees, thick lilies (left) and tree roots all provide shelter and protection for fish. These areas are even more popular with fish when the sun is bright or the water is very cold.

 TOP TIP
In rivers, look for "creases" in the current, where slow-moving water meets faster water. Fish like to sit in the slower water and watch for passing food.

RODS & REELS

*T*here are a confusing number of rods and reels to choose from. If you are just starting out, bring an experienced friend or adult who can help you shop for your gear. You can also talk to a local tackle dealer about what equipment is best for the fishing in your area.

RODS

There are rods to suit different types of fishing. Their names—such as a pike rod or a carp rod—usually tell you what fish they are best used for catching.

Most modern rods are made from carbon fiber. The rods come in two or three sections which you push together. Make sure that the rod rings are all in line!

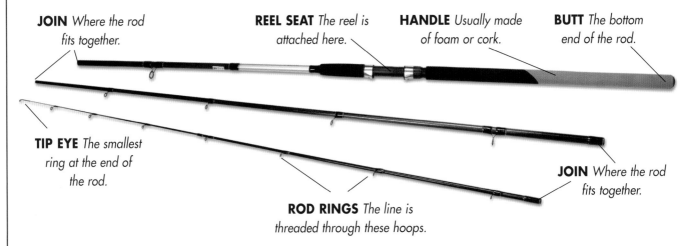

JOIN *Where the rod fits together.*

REEL SEAT *The reel is attached here.*

HANDLE *Usually made of foam or cork.*

BUTT *The bottom end of the rod.*

TIP EYE *The smallest ring at the end of the rod.*

JOIN *Where the rod fits together.*

ROD RINGS *The line is threaded through these hoops.*

REELS

There are three main types of reels: fixed spool, centerpins, and multipliers.

THE CENTERPIN *is a simple type of reel with a spool spinning freely on a spindle.*

Bale arm

THE MULTIPLIER REEL *is heavy-duty and good for fast retrieval. It is most often used in sea fishing.*

THE FIXED SPOOL *is the best all-around type of reel. The bale arm wraps line around the spool several times with each turn of the handle, and opens to allow* **casting***.*

HOW TO LOAD A FIXED SPOOL REEL

When loading a spool with line, make sure the line is within 1/8 inch (2-3 mm) of the edge of the spool. Load up at least 300 feet (100 m) of line.

STEP 1

Attach the reel to the rod at the reel seat.

Reel seat

STEP 2

Pass the line through the first rod ring.

STEP 3

Open the bale arm of the reel.

STEP 4

Push the button on the top of the spool and remove it.

STEP 5

Tie the line onto the spool and trim off the tag end.

STEP 7

Wind the line onto your spool, loading it to within 1/8 inch (2-3 mm) of the edge of the spool. Cut the line and thread it though the remaining rings.

STEP 6

Replace the spool onto the reel and close the bale arm.

TOP TIP

When winding the line on, keep it under tension by holding it with your spare hand between the reel and the rod ring. This makes sure the line is wound tightly and prevents tangles.

BAIT

Bait is anything you use to tempt a fish into biting the hook. Different species like to eat different things. Always match your hook size to your chosen bait. A big hook with a small bait won't get you many bites—big bait on a small hook won't hook you many fish!

SWEETCORN
This is a great bait, but fish learn to avoid it in heavily fished waters. Good for tench, bream, roach, rudd, carp and grayling.

PASTE
Fish may not see bait in muddy or cloudy water, so coat the bait in paste to give off extra scent.

DEADBAITS
Dead fish are standard baits used to catch pike and zander.

PELLETS
Often used as **loosefeed**, this is a great bait for species such as carp, tench, bream, barbel, catfish and chub.

DOG BISCUIT MIX
These float. On warm days carp will take them from the surface.

WORMS
Worms will help you catch any kind of fish.

CASTERS
Casters often attract better fish, especially roach, rudd and tench.

BREAD
This cheap and simple bait is one of the best there is for roach, rudd, tench, chub and carp.

GROUNDBAIT
A mix of cereals, breadcrumbs and other flavors.

TOP TIP
Whatever bait you use, make sure the hook's point is showing when you put it on, or you will miss bites.

LUNCHEON MEAT

An excellent bait for chub, barbel, carp, and tench, especially in colored water.

LURES

Lures are made from wood, plastic or metal. They are made to look like small fish that larger fish want to eat.

HEMP

Essential for loosefeed when fishing tench, roach, barbel, and carp.

MAGGOTS

All fish love maggots, from tiny roach to large carp!

BOILIES

These help avoid the smaller fish because they mainly attract larger carp, tench, bream, and barbel.

GROUNDBAIT

Groundbait is a mix of breadcrumbs, cereals and other attractive additives. This is mixed with water and put into the swim to attract fish and encourage them to feed. You can do this either by hand, catapult, or in a swimfeeder (see page 24).

To make groundbait, add water gradually to the dry mixture and mix well. It should squeeze together but break up easily.

Feeding is key to successful angling. You must add enough to keep fish in your swim, but not too much so they get full. You want a swim of hungry fish looking for their next mouthful. Then you can catch them!

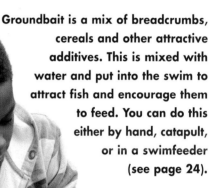

HOOKS & KNOTS

Hooks come in many sizes and shapes. The bigger the hook size number, the smaller the hook: a 20 is small, whereas a 6 is big.

TYPES OF HOOK

Spade-end hooks have a flattened area at the top. The knot sits below this area.
Eyed hooks have a small ring at the top. They are tied onto the line with the knot sitting above the eye.
Barbless hooks are easier to remove from a fish's mouth.
These are generally preferred over barbed hooks.

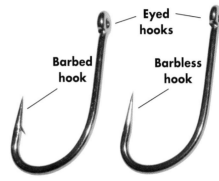
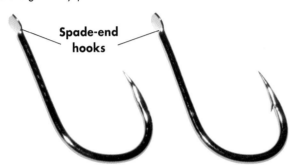

Spade-end hooks

Eyed hooks

Barbed hook

Barbless hook

KNOTS

A well-tied knot is essential.
Take your time when tying knots, and always moisten them with saliva before tightening.
Here are some of the best knots to use when fishing.

TYING A HOOKLENGTH – OVERHAND LOOP KNOT

A hooklength is the short piece of line connecting your hook to your main line.
Always use a lower breaking strain line than your main line in case you get snagged and have to pull for a break. This way you get all your tackle back except the hook.

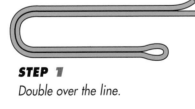

STEP 1
Double over the line.

STEP 2
Make a loop.

STEP 3
Pass the end through the loop twice.

STEP 4
Moisten with saliva, slowly tighten and trim off the tag.
Cut as much line as you need—about a foot (30 cm)—and tie on your hook with one of the following knots.

TOP TIP
A really sharp hook is the most important part of your tackle. Rest your hook point on a fingernail and gently pull down—if it digs in straight away, it's sharp. If it slides across your nail, toss it!

LOOP-TO-LOOP KNOT

Attaching a hooklength to your main line—the loop-to-loop knot.

STEP 1
Tie an overhand loop knot in your main line. Pass the hook (attached to the hooklength) through the main line loop.

Hooklength

Main line

STEP 2
Pass the hook through the hooklength loop.

STEP 3
Carefully pull to tighten the knot.

UNI OR GRINNER KNOT

Use this for larger fish with heavier monofilament or braid line.

STEP 1
Pass the line through the eye of the hook or swivel twice.

STEP 2
Now form a loop with the end of the line and pass it under both lines coming from the hook.

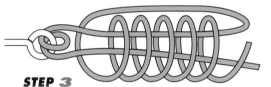

STEP 3
Pass the end down through the loop, around behind the two lines coming from the hook. Repeat this five times.

STEP 4
Moisten with saliva and tighten slowly. Pull the knot down to the eye of the hook or swivel and trim off the spare line or tag.

KNOTLESS KNOT

Use this for making hair-rigs, where the bait is held on a short piece of line tied to the bare hook. Perfect when carp, tench or bream fishing, with either braid or monofilament line.

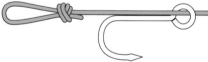

STEP 1
Tie a small loop in the hooklength material and thread your hook onto your hooklength.

STEP 2
Wrap the unlooped end of your hooklength around the hook twice.

STEP 3
Wrap the line around the hook five more times or until it is level with the hook point. Pass the end through the eye of the hook.

STEP 4
Tie a swivel on the other end using the grinner knot (above).

The swivel is a small metal device made of two rings and a pivoting central joint. Line is tied to the two ends. Because they can spin, it prevents the line from twisting and tangling.

FLOATS & WEIGHTS

Weights and floats work together to provide casting weight *and* tell you when you've got a bite. A float is a buoyant stick-like bite indicator with a bright tip. When attached to the line properly, it is the most sensitive indicator around!

Pinching a shot on to the line.

SPLIT-SHOT WEIGHTS

Split-shot **weights are pinched on to the line below the float. They make the float sit upright in the water.** *Split-shot come in different sizes from SSG (very big) to number 10 (very small).*

| SSG | AAA | BB | 1 | 4 | 6 | 8 |

STILLWATER FLOATS

Still water floats are attached to the line by the bottom end only. For this reason they are known as "wagglers."
When fishing with a waggler use a float adaptor. This is threaded on the line instead of the float. The float is then pushed into the adaptor's soft rubber sleeve. An adaptor allows you to swap floats quickly and easily without having to re-tackle.

Insert waggler
For close fishing in calm conditions.

Straight waggler
More stable than the insert waggler.

Bodied waggler
For fishing further out or in windy conditions.

DRENNAN PEACOCK 2½AA

Float adaptor
Allows for quick changes of floats.

A float rising in the water, dipping under water, or moving to the side indicates a bite.

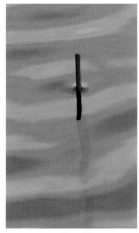

A waggler floating correctly in still water.

Different shotting patterns make the bait behave differently. Most of the shot for wagglers is around the bottom of the float to keep it stable. The rest is squeezed down the line to sink the bait to the right depth. This shot can be either all grouped together, known as "bulk," or placed "shirt-button" style, evenly spaced down the line.

As the weights fall through the water, they make the float settle. Bulk is used to get the bait down quickly to fish in deeper water. Shirt-button creates a gently falling bait for fish higher up in the water. The most important weights are "tell-tale" shots. These are placed close to the hook and are usually very small (number 8 or 10). With a pair of tell-tale shot four inches (ten cm) and eight inches (20 cm) from the hook, any tiny bites will move the float. You should strike after any movement of the float. Even a tiny lift means you've got a fish!

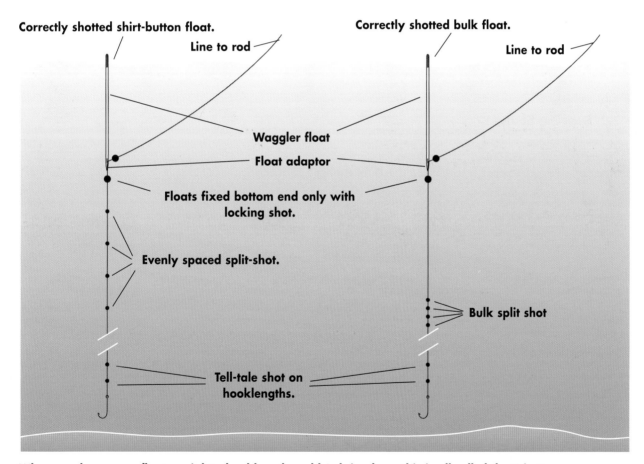

Correctly shotted shirt-button float.

Line to rod

Correctly shotted bulk float.

Line to rod

Waggler float

Float adaptor

Floats fixed bottom end only with locking shot.

Evenly spaced split-shot.

Bulk split shot

Tell-tale shot on hooklengths.

When you have your float, weights, hooklength and hook in place, this is all called the "rig."

TOP TIP

Watch how long it takes for the float to settle, including the last tell-tale shots. If the float doesn't settle, a fish has taken the bait as the line was sinking, so strike!

RIVER FLOATS & TROTTING

R iver floats are connected top and bottom by float rubbers. This way the floats are easier to control in running water.

FLOATS & FLOAT RUBBERS

Float rubbers stop your float from getting dragged under by the flowing river. Now you can stop the float from moving downstream and let your bait flutter attractively in the current. This technique is called "holding back."

Float rubbers
Little rubber bands which are used to hold river floats on the line.

Grayling floats
These are very traditional floats. They are made to be bouyant and visible in fast, broken water where grayling live.

Float rubber

Stick floats
These are delicate trotting floats, used for good presentation in slower, steadier flows.

Chubber floats
These are very buoyant and are perfect for big baits or when fishing in very fast water.

Avon floats
These are used in fast water. Their thin stem helps to keep them stable.

TROTTING

Trotting is float fishing in running water. The key is controling the float downstream.
As the float travels downstream, let out your line under slight tension. That way, the float travels a bit slower than the current. The river flow is much slower on the bottom than at the surface—now your bait is moving at the correct speed for fish near the bottom.

If the hook snags on the bottom, move the float down toward the hook a little. Now the hook is shallower. If the hook doesn't snag, try going a little deeper until you're presenting the bait just off the river bottom.

With practice, you can guide a float at just the right speed into the hotspots where the fish are feeding. It takes some skill, but it sure is exciting!

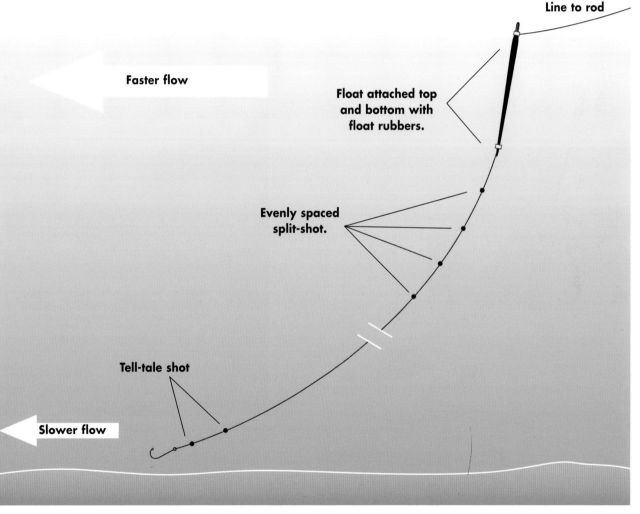

Line to rod

Faster flow

Float attached top
and bottom with
float rubbers.

Evenly spaced
split-shot.

Tell-tale shot

Slower flow

River float rig

TOP TIP
A float with lots of shot is much easier to control than a lighter float and helps the bait look more natural in the water. Don't be scared of using heavy floats!

CASTING

There are two main ways to cast – underarm for close-in fishing and overhead for further out.

CASTING UNDERARM

This is great for delicate, accurate close-in fishing where a big splash would scare fish. It is also perfect for flicking your bait into tricky spots, like under overhanging trees.

STEP 1

Open the bale arm on your reel and point your rod up. Let out enough line so that your rig is at waist height and you have two feet (60 cm) of line from the reel to your left hand.

Float

STEP 2

Swing the rig back toward you.

STEP 3

Lower the rod tip, flick the rig toward the water and let go of the line.

Float

Float

STEP 4

Just before the rig lands, stop the line coming off the reel with your right middle finger. This ensures that it hits the water gently in a straight line. Close the bale arm when the rig has landed.

TOP TIP
If you can, cast further out than you need to, then slowly reel back in to your spot. This way you are less likely to frighten the fish.

This is used when you need to cast further out.

Float

STEP 1

Open the bale arm on your reel and let out some line so there is about a three-foot (one-meter) drop between rod tip and rig.

STEP 2

Hold the rod with your left hand at the bottom of the handle and the right gripping the reel seat. Hook the line over your right index finger.

Float

STEP 3

With the rod behind you at a 45° angle, pull on your left hand and use the right hand as a pivot.

STEP 4

When the rod gets to 45° in front of you, release the line from your right finger.

STEP 5

Just before the rig lands, use your right index finger to "feather" the line. This is done by gently pressing on the spool with your finger. Feathering lands the rig slowly in a straight line. When it hits the water, stop the spool with your finger and close the bale arm.

LANDING A FISH

Whehen you think you've got a bite, you need to get the hook into the fish's mouth. This is called striking. You strike by moving the rod quickly but smoothly up or to the side. Then you need to land, unhook, and release the fish as quickly as possible.

LAND, UNHOOK, AND RELEASE

Before fishing, set the reel's clutch to let out line under pressure. Otherwise your line will snap when you hook a monster fish!

Clutch

STEP 1
If it's a small fish, you can carefully reel it in.

STEP 2
Gently swing the fish to your hand.

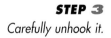

STEP 3
Carefully unhook it.

STEP 4
Slip it back into the water.

You need to tire out bigger fish before reeling them in. Hold the rod up to wear the fish out. If it heads for a reedbed or other snag, use sidestrain—pulling sideways in the opposite direction—to keep it clear.

Reel in and lower the rod tip. Use the rod to pull the fish in. When the fish is tired and close, hold the landing net underwater. Draw the fish over the net, then lift it up.

Carry the fish in the net to your wet unhooking mat.

Remove the hook by pulling gently on the bend.

USING A DISGORGER

Unfortunately, a fish may sometimes swallow a hook. If that happens you can easily retrieve it and harmlessly release the fish by using a disgorger. **Different ones are needed depending on the hook size. Carry several disgorgers just in case.**

STEP 1
Hold the fish firmly but gently with the line fairly tight so that it's between your hand and the hook.

STEP 2
Hook the disgorger onto the line and slide it down into the fish's mouth. Push down gently against the hookhold to release the hook.

STEP 3
Pull the disgorger and hook out, and release the fish.

TOP TIP
If you want to weigh the fish, place it carefully in a wet weigh sling and hang it on your scales. Make sure all its fins are flat against its body. If you want a photo, hold the fish low to the ground and smile!

LEGERING

Legering means using a weight or swimfeeder to place a pile of bait on the bottom of the river or lake. There is no float on the line, but there is a bite indicator on or attached to the rod. Legering is normally used to present a still bait. It is better used for distance fishing rather than float fishing.

SWIMFEEDERS

A swimfeeder is a plastic container with holes in it.

It is used to attract bottom-feeding fish to the area you are fishing. Swimfeeders can be used in place of a leger weight. There are two types of swimfeeder: a maggot feeder and an open-end feeder.

The maggot feeder is filled with maggots before each cast.

The maggots crawl out on the river or lake bottom drawing fish to your hookbait. Accurate casting is essential with this feeder. You must hit the same area each time to build up a bed of feed.

Maggot feeders

An open-ended feeder is filled with groundbait before each cast. The groundbait is deposited on the bottom near your hookbait, just as with a maggot feeder.

Accurate casting is also needed with this feeder. Recast every 15 minutes, making sure you hit the same spot every time. It may take a while, but eventually fish will be drawn to your groundbait, and you'll start catching!

Open-end feeder

Main line

Plastic bead

Link swivel

Weight

Hooklength

RUNNING LEGER

A running leger is a weight moving freely on the main line. A swivel and a plastic or rubber bead stops the weight from sliding down to the hook. You tie your hooklength to the swivel in this rig.
When a fish takes the bait, it pulls the line through the **run ring** *connected to the weight. This indicates a bite!*

BOLT RIGS

Bolt rigs are a way of legering with heavy weights.
The fish sucks in a bait and swims off. The heavy weight pulls the hook into their mouth making them "bolt" or swim away sharply. You don't need to strike—the fish is already hooked! Bolt rigs are often used when waiting long periods while fishing for **specimen** *carp, tench and bream.*

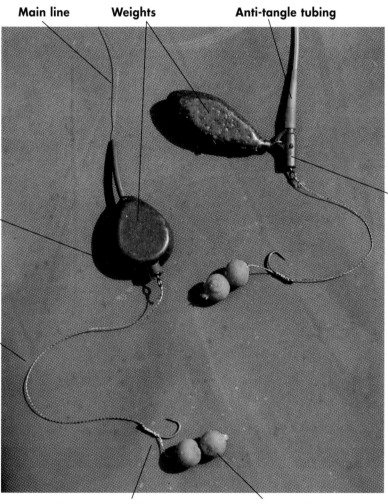

Main line **Weights** **Anti-tangle tubing**

Swivel pushed into rubber sleeve.

Lead clip

Hooklength made of soft braid.

Hook tied on with knotless knot. **Hair-rigged bait**

TOP TIP
Bolt rigs must be safe. If your line snaps after a fish has been hooked, the weight must be able to fall off the rig. Otherwise the fish would have to drag the weight around everywhere.

INDICATORS

There are no floats on a leger rig, but there are plenty of other gadgets to show when you have hooked a fish. These are sensitive attachments for the end of your rod or your line that move when a fish is hooked.

QUIVERTIP

A quivertip is a fine, sensitive rod tip which quivers, knocks or pulls around when a fish has taken the bait.

Quivertips are often used when fishing for smaller species. They can be made of fiberglass or carbon. Fiberglass tips are delicate and move softly; carbon tips are stiffer and more powerful.

Bites are indicated by movement of the tip.

Rod rest

Quivertipping is usually used on rivers and still waters with either a running leger or swimfeeders (see pages 24-25). After casting, the rod is placed on a rest parallel to the bank with a 90° angle between the quivertip and line. The line tightened slowly until there is a tiny bend in the tip. In still waters, have the tip as close to the water as possible for maximum indication. In a river, point the rod upward, so as much line as possible is out of the flow.

Bobbins are very versatile and can be used with any leger set-up. *They are most often used when fishing for larger fish in still waters. Once you have cast out, the rod is placed in two rests, sometimes with a **bite alarm**. The bobbin is clipped onto the line between the reel and the front rest. It should hang about midway from the rod to the ground.*

Bobbin

Bobbin

Bobbin

*If a fish takes the bait and moves toward you, you get a "**drop-back** bite," where the bobbin drops to the ground.*

If the fish swims away from you, the bobbin rises to the rod.

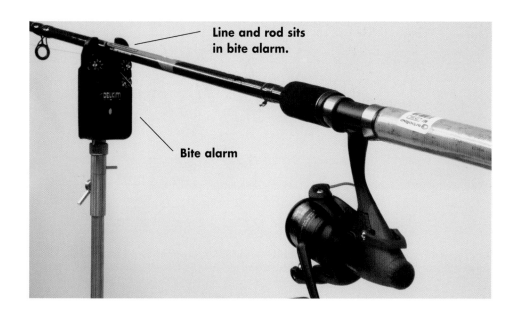

Line and rod sits in bite alarm.

Bite alarm

Bite alarms, or "buzzers," take the place of the front rod rest. They beep when the line is pulled over a small wheel or vibrating plate.

EQUIPMENT

Fly fishing is a way of presenting an imitation "fly" to catch fish like trout or salmon. This style can also be used to catch coarse fish and even sea fish. There are thousands of different flies—each one is designed to look like a land or sea creature that fish eat. It is a very active and mobile fishing style. If you haven't tried it yet, you really should—it's great fun!

FLY FISHING EQUIPMENT

six ft six in (two m) number 2 rod

Bag

Tapered leader
A length of monofilament line which is thick at one end and tapers down to a thin, delicate end. The thick end is attached to the fly line. The fly is tied to the thin end.

Reels
It is useful to have different types of lines and reels.

Braided loop connectors
This is used to connect your fly line to your tapered leader.

Folding landing net

Ten foot (three-meter) number 7/8 rod
Every rod has an AFTM rating–this matches the weight of the line that the rod will work with.

Floatant
To keep dry flies floating.

Priest
If you are catching trout to eat, this is used to humanely knock them on the head.

Sinkant
To help sink leaders.

Line for tippets
The short length of light line at the end of a leader.

Flies
Dry flies, wet flies, nymphs, and buzzers.

TOP TIP
The best all-around set-up for fly fishing is a nine-foot (2.7 m) number 6 rod, cheap reel, and a decent number 6 WF, F (weight forward, floating) line.

STEP 1
Attach the reel
to the rod.

STEP 2
Attach a braided
loop to the end of the
fly line. Simply thread
the line into the hollow
braid and slip the
sleeve over the join.

STEP 3
Thread the fly line through
the eyes.

STEP 4
Take a tapered leader and
tie a loop in the thickest end.

STEP 5
Attach the leader to the braided loop with
the loop-to-loop knot (see page 15).

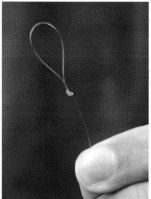

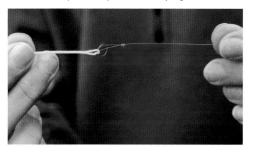

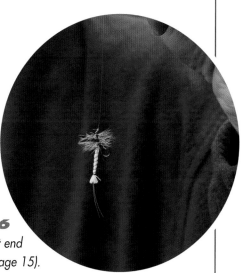

STEP 6
Tie your chosen fly to the tippet (the thinnest end
section of the leader) with a grinner knot (see page 15).

The fly line is very important. Try to spend as much as you can on it.

Cheap lines have bad "memory," meaning they end up in tight coils after being stored on the reel.

There are several types of fly line:

Double taper (DT) These have a long body section with each end tapering to a fine point — good for delicate presentations.

Weight forward (WF) These have a thin body section with a thicker end before tapering to a point — good for casting further.

Shooting head (SH) These are half the length of normal fly lines and are attached to thin backing line — great for real distance casting.

The sink rate of the fly line is the speed the line sinks through the water.
You can buy anything from floating right up to fast–sinking fly lines.

SINK RATE

Floating These float on the surface of the water.	**Intermediate** These sink very, very slowly.
Sink tip These float, except for the last one to two meters which slowly sink.	**Slow, Medium,** or **Fast Sinking** These sink at different rates through the water.

CASTING

Fly rods are very flexible and can store lots of energy. The fly line is also the rod's casting weight. When the line bends the rod ready for casting, it's called "loading the rod." Timing here is more important than strength, so practice casting often.

CASTING

When casting a fly you make several "false casts" before the final cast.

On each false forward cast, a little more line is released, until you have enough line to reach the required distance.

The correct grip.

STEP 1
Pull off enough line for the cast.

STEP 2
Make a back cast. Keep your wrist straight, and move your arm sharply backward so the rod tip gets to the one o'clock position, then stop abruptly. This loads the rod with the weight of the line.

STEP 3
Pause. When the line has straightened out behind you and loaded the rod, move your arm forward sharply to the 11 o'clock position. Let two feet (60 cm) of line out with your left hand. Pause again to let the line straighten and load the rod.

STEP 4

Repeat these false casts until enough line is out. Remember to pause each time to let the line to load the rod. Keep your wrist straight!

Straight wrist

STEP 5

On the final forward cast, let go of the line with your left hand. As it falls to the water's surface, lower the rod tip to waist height.

Once you've mastered these basics, you can start to get more advanced. When delivering the final cast on a river, try wiggling the rod tip as the line shoots out. This makes the line land in a wiggle, and allows the current to move it in a more natural way. It also gives a fish more time to take the bait.

TOP TIP
Do not allow the fly or line to touch the water until your final cast, or you will spook the fish.

DRY FLY FISHING

Dry fly fishing is often considered to be the most skillful style of fly fishing. This style requires careful observation and accurate presentation. Dry flies imitate adult land or newborn insects on the surface of the water. A floating line is used. It can be useful to have some floatant to apply to dry flies, to keep them afloat. The best time of day for dry fly fishing is often the evening, when there are usually lots of flies hatching.

ON LAKES

Dry fly fishing on lakes is often a case of being there at the right time. For example, a sudden hatch of aquatic insects, or a gusty wind carrying insects into the lake, can cause trout to rise to the surface and feed.

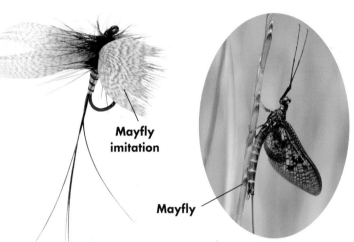

Mayfly
imitation

Mayfly

Casting should be kept to a minimum. You need to be stealthy. Trout often come very close to the bank if they are undisturbed. This will make them easier to catch. Keep your fly as static as possible, and strike as soon as it is taken by a fish.

**Static dry
fly fishing.**

TOP TIP
You want your fly to float but your tippet to sink so there's no line silhouette on the surface. Rub some de-greaser onto the tippet to stop it from floating.

When dry fly fishing on a river, start looking for fish at the most downstream spot you can. Stealthily work your way upstream, watching and listening for rising trout. This way the fish won't see you.

When you see a rising fish, wait and watch. Usually it will rise again in exactly the same spot. Next, figure out what it is eating. You should easily be able to see what flies are being eaten. Tie a fly to your line and cast upstream, just above where you saw the fish rise. Hopefully the hungry fish will take it and you'll have a bite!

Cast upstream so that the fly lands just above the spot where the fish rose. Now wait—good luck!

NYMPH FISHING

Nymphs are aquatic insects still in their underwater stage before they become adults. Sub-surface nymphs are a large part of a trout's diet. Fishing with imitation nymphs can be very successful, but it is also challenging. The trout have plenty of time to decide whether or not your "nymph" is real!

ON LAKES

Nymph fishing in lakes is often fishing "blind." You can't see the trout like you can when they're rising to take dry flies.

Getting the fly to the right depth is very important. Start by fishing as close to the bottom as possible. Use either a sinking line or a floating line with a long leader and weighted fly. Always imagine a fish is following your fly, and try to tempt it with the way you retrieve the line. You can use small fast twitches, long slow pulls, or a figure 8 retrieve.

FIGURE 8 RETRIEVE

STEP 1
Pinch the line between your thumb and index finger.

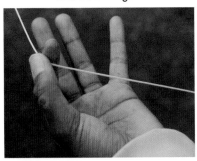

STEP 2
Loop the line around your index finger and your little finger.

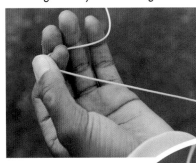

STEP 3
Pull your little finger down to make a loop.

STEP 4
Grab the line from your little finger with your thumb and index finger.

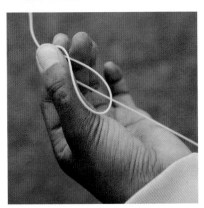

STEP 5
Repeat this process to retrieve in a figure 8.

TOP TIP
**On overcast or warm days, trout are likely to be near the surface.
On bright or cold days, they are often near or on the bottom.**

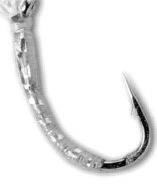

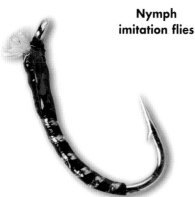

Nymph imitation flies

ON RIVERS

There are two ways of nymph fishing a river — upstream or downstream.

To nymph fish upstream, use a floating line and allow the fly to drift back in the river flow. Take up the slack line with your spare hand. To get the right depth, either use a weighted fly or squeeze one or two small split-shots onto your tippet.

If the leader or fly line stops or acts strangely, strike! Takes are often gentle, so stay alert.

Fishing downstream is easier at first because takes are obvious. Still, the fly looks unnatural as the current sweeps it along. Try fishing upstream if you can. Once you've mastered these difficult skills, you'll catch far more trout.

Nymph fishing downstream

TOP TIP
Explore the river — travel light and try as many new spots as you can.

EQUIPMENT

What could be more thrilling than casting into the mighty sea? There are a lot of exciting locations to fish from — a sandy beach, a rocky outcrop, a pier, or even a boat. With some basic understanding of tides, weather, casting, and safety, you'll soon be enjoying the challenges of sea fishing.

SEA EQUIPMENT

Sea fishing tackle must be strong enough to withstand powerful waves and tides.

12 foot (4 m) Beachcaster rod

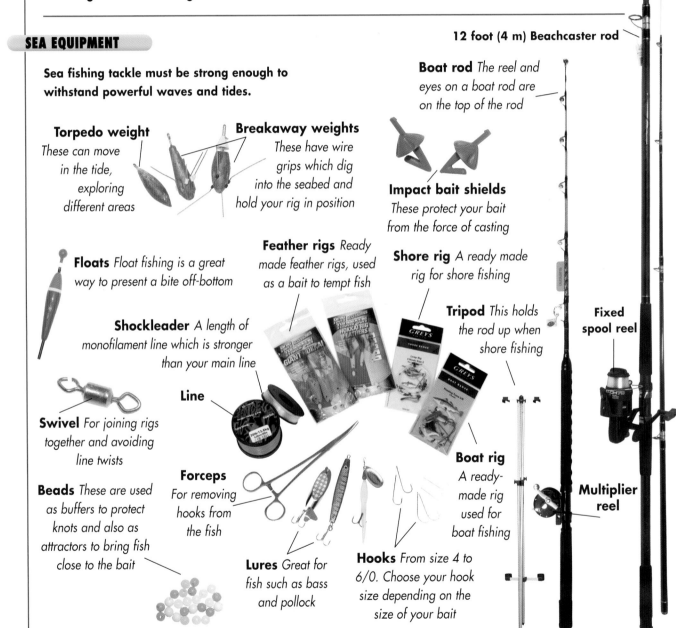

Torpedo weight These can move in the tide, exploring different areas

Breakaway weights These have wire grips which dig into the seabed and hold your rig in position

Boat rod The reel and eyes on a boat rod are on the top of the rod

Impact bait shields These protect your bait from the force of casting

Floats Float fishing is a great way to present a bite off-bottom

Feather rigs Ready made feather rigs, used as a bait to tempt fish

Shore rig A ready made rig for shore fishing

Shockleader A length of monofilament line which is stronger than your main line

Tripod This holds the rod up when shore fishing

Fixed spool reel

Line

Swivel For joining rigs together and avoiding line twists

Forceps For removing hooks from the fish

Boat rig A ready-made rig used for boat fishing

Multiplier reel

Beads These are used as buffers to protect knots and also as attractors to bring fish close to the bait

Lures Great for fish such as bass and pollock

Hooks From size 4 to 6/0. Choose your hook size depending on the size of your bait

 TOP TIP
Salt can corrode. After every trip, wash your rod with warm water and a little soap. Then rinse your reel under warm water.

Bait can quickly spoil, especially on warm days. Keep it fresh by keeping it in the shade in a cool box or in a bucket of sea water (change the water regularly.)

Ragworm *A great all-around bait*

King ragworm *These big worms can tempt some big fish!*

Mackerel strips *Cut into strips, mackerel is a very good bait for larger predators, such as bass, rays, tope, and conger eels.*

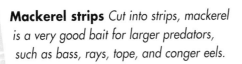

Razor fish *An excellent bait for flatfish, such as flounder*

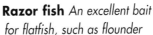

Feathers *Mackerel find these irresistible*

Squid *A tough bait often used to keep softer baits like worms on the hook. Alone, it is a good bait for cod and bass.*

Shore crabs *A great bait for bass, rays, and cod*

Lugworm *Nearly every sea fish will take a lugworm*

SHORE FISHING

Shore fishing is always exciting. Usual tackle is a 12-foot (four-meter) beachcaster rod, a multiplier reel with 15-20 lb (seven- to nine-kg) line, and a shockleader. The best places to cast from include sand and mud beds, between rocks, deeper holes, and gutters, around wooden *groins,* and channels between rocky and weedy areas.

When shore or pier fishing the rod is held almost upright, sometimes with a tripod. A bite is indicated by the rod's tip knocking or bending over. When float fishing, the float gets pulled under when you've got a bite, so strike!

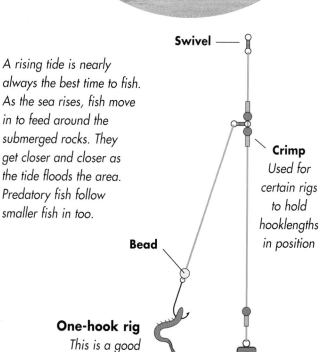

A rising tide is nearly always the best time to fish. As the sea rises, fish move in to feed around the submerged rocks. They get closer and closer as the tide floods the area. Predatory fish follow smaller fish in too.

Swivel

Crimp
Used for certain rigs to hold hooklengths in position

Bead

One-hook rig
This is a good streamlined rig for distance casting.

Lead weight

TOP TIP

**Never run on rocks, they can be wet and dangerous.
Always wear good shoes with lots of grip,
and always fish with a friend.**

PIER FISHING

Many anglers begin sea fishing by lowering a bait over their local pier. It's a great place both for catching fish and watching the experts.

Piers attract fish, so all you need to do is lower a bait. You don't even need to cast!
It is easier to fish the downtide side of a pier, but you will catch far more fish from the uptide side. Use a heavy breakaway weight to hold your rig in position. Aim to get your bait close to gutters. On wooden piers, fish next to one of the pier supports.

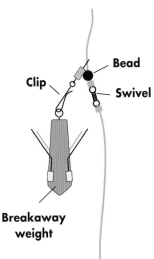

Bead

Clip

Swivel

Breakaway weight

Running rig
Most fish feed on the bottom. This simple running rig, with a single hook, is best when pier fishing.

TOP TIP
At low tide, look for any gullies, rocks, holes, snags or other features below the pier. These will be the best spots to cast when you return to fish at high tide.

CASTING

*C*asting is a skill which is most useful when fishing from the shore. You need to propel your bait out into the sea where the fish are feeding.

THE OFF GROUND CAST

For long-distance casting use the off ground cast. It gets its name because the rig is laid on the ground behind you before the cast is made.

STEP 1

Face where you want to cast, then twist around so you are facing behind you. Put your weight on your back foot.
The rod should be about 60° further around. Lay the rig on the ground 90° to the direction of the rod.
The distance from the rig to the rod tip should be at least half the length of your rod.

Weight on back foot.

Rig

STEP 2

Open the bale arm and hold the line with your index finger.

STEP 3

Twist back around starting with your head and ending with your arms. As you do this, slowly raise the rod tip. This action compresses the rod and builds up energy. Pull your left elbow up and through (if you are right-handed). Transfer your weight onto both feet.

Turn your body back around.

Weight on both feet.

STEP 4

When your right arm is at full extension above your head, pull your left arm back. The rod tip passes over your head. Put your weight onto your front foot to add power.

Move weight onto front foot.

STEP 5

Release the line when the rod is fully loaded.
Point the rod where you want the rig to land!

POLLUTION

Fishing is about being close to nature, and so you must be responsible. Don't leave garbage or old line around when you have finished fishing. Follow any specific rules on the lakes or rivers that you visit. Anglers are the guardians of the countryside. Often they are the only people to visit many remote natural areas. Be sure to report any instances of harmed wildlife or pollution you may come across. You will find a pollution hotline phone number on your fishing license.

No one wants to fish in a pond or river like this, so always clean up any litter or old line when you leave.

LICENSES & RULES

*F*or coarse and fly fishing in the U.S. and Canada, every angler over a certain age needs a fishing license. The age limits change from state to state and province to province — check your local area's fishing license website. So why buy a license? Not only is it the law, all money from fishing license sales helps protect the sport. Governments use this money to clean the waters, fund hatcheries to keep fish populations healthy, and much more!

United Sates
Coastal U.S. states have one set of rules for freshwater fishing and another for saltwater.
Some states have closed seasons but usually only for certain species, and with no differentiation between still and running water. Each state has a rule about how many rods an angler can use at once. Licenses are available from larger fishing supply stores.

You are free to fish on almost any public land, but private land is by permission only. The water is not owned though, so if there is any public access to launch a boat, you are free to fish the entire lake or river as long as you are on the water.

United Kingdom
Here, a fishing license is known as a rod license, because it is the rod that is licensed, not the angler!
You need permission to fish from whoever owns the water. This usually means a day ticket, where you pay a one-off fee for a day's fishing, or a season ticket, where you pay a larger fee to be able to fish an area for a whole year. You can also join a club. This gives you access to a few different areas and you can come and go as you please! Joining a club or buying a season ticket works out to be less expensive than buying many of day tickets.

On rivers, there is a closed season between March 15 and June 15. On canals and still waters, it is up to the landowner whether to enforce a closed season.

Sea fishing is different, you don't need any licenses to fish in the sea, and there is no closed season.

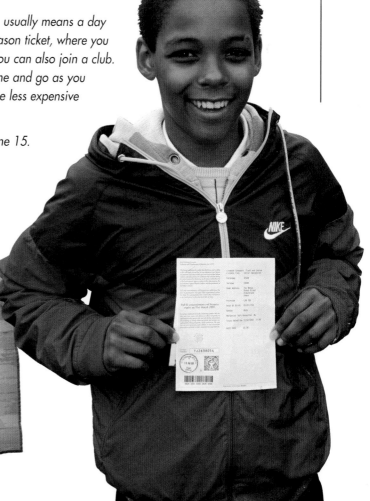

RULES
No fishing without a license.

No fishing underneath power lines.

Do not leave any litter.

If you find any litter take it home with you!

Do not enter the water to get things you have dropped.

DIET & FITNESS

A lot of fishing is very active, and many of the best anglers are those who put a lot of effort into their fishing. You'll be surprised at how fit fishing keeps you!

A healthy balanced diet is important when fishing. You'll be doing a lot of walking, climbing and, creeping around, so you'll need energy from your food to keep you going. This pie chart shows you the percentages of foods that should be eaten to maintain a balanced diet.

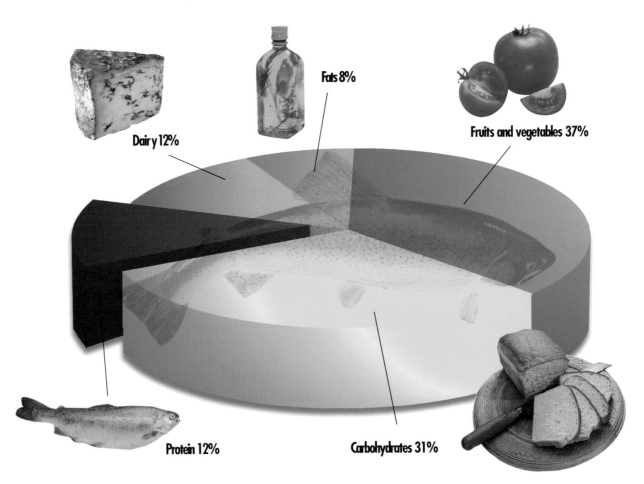

Fats 8%

Dairy 12%

Fruits and vegetables 37%

Protein 12%

Carbohydrates 31%

Always carry plenty of fresh water, especially in summer, and enough food for your day out.
Sandwiches keep you full, and snacks like fruit are useful for an energy boost. If you are night fishing, nothing beats a small stove for making hot food and drinks!

If you do a lot of fishing, pick up a good, portable adjustable chair.

SAFETY

Being in the middle of nature next to water can be risky. As long as you stay smart, there's no reason anything should go wrong. It's a good idea to go fishing with a friend or two, and not just for safety. You'll need someone to photograph your new personal best catch for you! It's also worth taking a cell phone, just in case you need to contact anyone. Some out-of-the-way fishing spots have limited network coverage though, so don't just rely on the phone to be safe.

Tell at least one person where you're going and what time you'll be back. It only takes a few seconds and it might be important that you did.

If it's going to be dusk or dark when you come home, make sure you take a flashlight and spare batteries. Walk carefully.

Be careful at the water's edge or when out in boats. It's possible to drown in just a few inches of water. If you do go out in a boat, always wear a lifejacket.

Finally, be aware of overhead power lines. Never fish directly underneath them. Most rods are made of carbon, which is an excellent conductor of electricity. A shock through a fishing rod is enough to kill. When walking under power lines, keep your rods parallel with the ground. A rod doesn't need to actually touch the lines to conduct the electricity. Stay sensible, and you'll stay safe!

Be aware of overhead power lines.

HOW THE PROS DO IT

Being a successful angler means different things to different people. It could be winning a lot of money in high-pressure fishing tournaments or patiently outwitting the biggest, craftiest fish. What all good anglers have in common though is a thoughtful approach. They are able to solve problems and pay close attention to the weather and conditions. Here are some of the most successful anglers in the history of the sport. Read on, but remember, if you go fishing and enjoy yourself, that's a success too!

ROLAND MARTIN

Roland Martin is a professional U.S. sport angler, fishing primarily for bass in tournaments.

He is very successful, having won many competitions and been invited into the Professional Bass Fishing Hall of Fame, the International Game Fish Association Hall of Fame, and the Freshwater Fishing Hall of Fame. He also hosts the TV show, "Fishing with Roland Martin."

GEORGINA BALLANTYNE

Fishing is a great sport for men and women.

On October 7, 1922, Georgina Ballantyne caught the biggest salmon ever recorded in the UK – and it's still the record! The huge 64-lb (29-kg) River Tay fish took ten hours to land. It is reported that the salmon was so big a pony and cart was needed to get the fish home!

Thought to be the most influential angler in living memory, Richard (Dick) Walker revolutionized the sport.

He was the first person to say that big fish – especially carp – could be caught by design. Before him, carp were considered impossible to catch! There wasn't any specialized tackle when he started fishing, so he designed and made his own. This included bite alarms, rods, flies, and Arlesey bomb weights. Some of his Mark IV split cane rods are still in use today. They are extremely expensive!

Matt Hayes is probably the UK's best-known fishing celebrity.

He was 30 when he gave up his successful office job to launch a career in fishing. He has fished all over the world and caught all kinds of fish, even great white sharks. To Hayes, the mystery and excitement of fishing are more important than the size and weight of the catch. Hayes won the Drennan Cup (specimen fishing's top prize) in 1998. Since then he has left big fish angling behind to explore different locations and methods of fishing.

GLOSSARY

BITE ALARM – *An electronic device which beeps when a fish pulls line over a small wheel or vibration sensor*

BOBBIN – *A method of bite indication. A bobbin clips and hangs on the line between the reel and rod rest, rising or falling when a fish takes the bait*

BOILIE – *Flavored and nutritious paste baits which are rolled into balls and boiled. Often used for carp fishing*

BOLT RIG – *A leger rig using a heavy weight to cause fish to "bolt" and hook themselves*

BRAID – *Main line or hooklength material which is very low in diameter for its breaking strain and has no stretch. It is not very abrasion resistant however, take care if using it around snags.*

CASTING – *Using a rod to throw bait or a fly into water*

CASTING WEIGHT – *The total weight (made up of split-shot or leger weights) needed to cast the rig the required distance*

CLOSE-IN – *Fishing close to the bank*

DISGORGER – *A pencil-like item with a slit in one end. It is used to remove hooks from fish*

DROP-BACK – *During legering, when a fish takes the bait and swims toward you, causing the bobbin to drop back instead of going up*

FORCEPS – *An unhooking tool for pike and zander fishing*

GROINS – *A low wall or sturdy timber barrier built out into the sea from a beach*

GROUNDBAIT – *A mix of crumb and cereals with flavors and additives. It is mixed with water until fluffy, squeezed together and thrown in the water to attract fish and encourage them to feed*

HAIR-RIG – *A way of presenting a bait (often a boilie) so it is not directly on the hook. This gets more bites from wary fish and improves hooking. The bait is held on a short piece of line attached to the hook*

HOOKLENGTH – *A length of line used to connect your hook to your main line*

LOOSEFEED – *Bait that you can throw into the water to attract fish to feed in a certain area*

LURE – *Any "bait" which imitates natural, living creatures that fish eat*

MONOFILAMENT – *Normal nylon fishing line*

RUN RING – *This ring has a wide bore allowing a fish to pull the line through without feeling resistance*

SPECIMEN – *A large fish of a certain species*

SPLIT-SHOT – *A small weight attached to the line when float fishing*

TAPERED LEADER – *A length of monofilament line that is thick at one end and thin at the other end*

UNHOOKING MAT – *A padded mat used to put fish on while they are being unhooked. It protects the fish from rough ground*

INDEX